AF882140

WHAT IS THIS PLACE?

A Realtor's Tour

of the Emerson Street House

By Activist Author
Diane Freaney

Author Photo by Julie Keefe

House Photos Jen Sotolongo

ISBN: 978-1-957365-12-1 paperback

Published by Emerson House Press
www.dianefreaney.com

INTRODUCTION

I purchased the property at 1006 NE Emerson Street from a goat farmer who needed the equity out of her rental property so she could build a new barn for her goats. I learned that the house on the property was built without permits and attention to building codes, a common practice in Northeast Portland, Oregon in the day. I attempted to remodel the house first. When it became evident that a remodel was not viable, I dreamed of a new vision.

My father had a stroke eight months before he passed, from which he never fully recovered. Dr. Roy Cacciaguida, my parents' doctor for many years, told me to find an Assisted Living / Skilled Nursing Facility. Neither parent had handled my father's stroke appropriately and they could not continue to live alone.

My father planned for my mother and himself to Age at Home. He purchased a condo in an over 55 community ten years before he was ready to sell their single-family home and move in. He served on the Condominium Association Board so he could assure the community was well-managed and well-maintained. He always envisioned himself as the caregiver for my mother. He never imagined he would become incapacitated by a stroke and unable to care for himself or my mother.

My parents moved to Brighton Gardens by Marriott in West Palm Beach. The year was 1997; the building was new, the staff was caring and professional, and the residents were happy and social. The problem: it wasn't profitable so cost cutting over time took its toll and eventually Marriott sold Brighton Gardens.

On my birthday, September 15, 2017, an article in the Palm Beach Post caught my eye, "We Averted a Catastrophe: Seniors Wilted at West Palm Home Post-Irma."

Oh my God, that is where my parents lived until their passing. Thanks to the West Palm Beach police and fire, all residents survived. What is deeply distressing is the lack of empathy and caring demonstrated by the management. Brighton Gardens had gone from a shiny new model, designed to provide quality end of life care to a place to warehouse the old and infirm in just 20 years.

Bricks and mortar can be beautiful and environmentally sustainable as built. But then what? Who lives there or works there or plays there? How is the experience for these folks? Do these buildings solve problems like homelessness, displacement, gentrification, affordable housing, healthcare? Or do these buildings create new problems?

Armed with my new MBA in Sustainable Systems from Bainbridge Graduate School (BGI) and cash from my recently liquidated Wall Street investments, I decided to invest My Own Money (MOM) to answer some of these questions.

TABLE OF CONTENTS

LIVING BUILDING CHALLENGE

Jason F. McLennan taught the Certificate Program in Green Building at Bainbridge Graduate Institute, the second year of BGI's MBA Program in Sustainable Systems. Those were heady times for Green Building in Seattle, Washington.

Jason was consulting on the Bullitt Center, a commercial office building at the intersection of the Central District neighborhood, and Capitol Hill, Seattle, Washington. It was officially opened on Earth Day, April 22, 2013. The Bullitt Center was designed to be the greenest commercial building in the world, and was certified as a "Living Building" by the International Living Future Institute—which was founded by Jason F. McLennan.

On the bullittcenter.org web site, the Bullitt Center declares that the lifespan of building is 250 years. Yet less than ten years later, everything had changed. Work / Live / Eat / Play / Pray has become a reality for most families. The Big Tech Five (Amazon, Apple, Facebook, Google, Microsoft) all have built huge office complexes to accommodate their huge staffs. But employees came to love remote work first thrust upon them by the pandemic.

The "Living Building" certification by the International Living Future Institute is a point in time, yet a Living Building must constantly adapt to changes in the world around it in order to actually be a Living Building.

The Emerson Street House was conceived as a Passive Net Zero house. The concept appealed to me, but I really didn't totally comprehend what that meant. I thought the Original Building Team understood my vision but I soon learned they were more adept at gaslighting that construction. They were taking the little old lady with the money (me) for a long expensive ride. From this point forward I will refer to the Original Building Team as OBT since they have resigned from the Living Building Challenge.

I will list the folks who have volunteered their time to help with the Living Building Challenge. These folks have moved on to important work in Northeast Portland and other communities.

EMC Charles Waylan Rogers ("Chuck"), Navy Seal (retired) and Vietnam Vet, my breakfast buddy at Aunt D's Diner in Stuart Florida, has volunteered to help with the final report for the Living Building Challenge and the Living Community Challenge.

LIVING COMMUNITY CHALLENGE

The Living Community Challenge is an extension of the Living Building Challenge. The Emerson Street House was built to accommodate many different community meetings. Both in the back usually referred to as the Accessory Dwelling Unit (ADU) and the Main House which was conceived as the main community space as long as I lived there.

Murthy Srinivas, BGI Classmate, convinced me to sign up for the Living Building / Living Community Challenge. Murthy was mentoring Marisa Hagney, a brilliant young woman, who epitomized the vision for the Living Building Living Community Challenge. Marisa left the International Living Future Institute, shortly after we met at The Emerson Street House. Marisa assured me that her ILFI colleagues would provide the support I needed.

INTERNATIONAL PASSIVE HOUSE CONFERENCE 2018 IN MUNICH, GERMANY

The Emerson Street House was the only International Living Future Institute, Living Building Challenge / Living Community Challenge to Exhibit at the International Passive House Conference in Munich, Germany.

Volunteer Project Managers, Mia Sheperd and Irish Gomm, hustled to design and build a first-class exhibit on a shoe string budget. Mia flew in from her consulting assignment in Rwanda, arriving just in time to join Irish at the Exhibit Hall and help her set up the exhibit.

Mia and Iris gifted me with the centerpiece of their Exhibit for The Emerson Street House, something I will always treasure.

EMERSON ST. HOUSE

1006 EMERSON ST. PORTLAND, OR

Communities are **people**. Buildings are **shelter**.

Meet the owner | DIANE FREANEY

Diane Freaney is a 73 year old, hard working, intelligent woman working to find solutions. Diane learned about Net Zero, High-Performing Buildings during the second year of her MBA at BGI/Pinchot, now Presidio Graduate School. She continued to have a prestigious education that supported her through her finances and to be financially successful. *But what about all the folks suffering* - tenants evited, mortgage foreclosure, more houseless folks on the street, more mental illness, more negative emotions and unhappiness.

Diane started Rooted Investing in 2013 as a way to give back to her community. She developed the Emerson St. House after Rooted Investing had started.

The house is designed to easily adapt to different uses - live/work, studio, gallery, event space, elder(s) alone or with caregiver(s), families with children and often several uses at the same time.

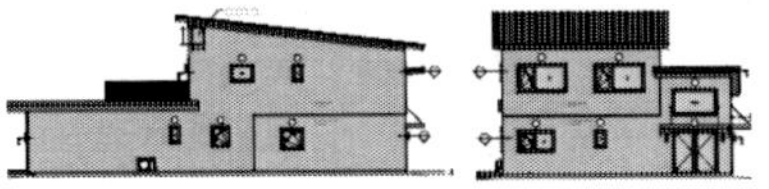

ESH is Passive House because there were saved costs on solar panels and to reach highest possible performing retrofit.

Area: 2,098 SF	Gallery 1,290 SF | ADU 808 SF
Envelope Specs:	Window [illegible]
	Wall Insulation [illegible]
	Heated Slab [illegible] (unheated)
Recycled Materials:	Cork Wall Insulation
	Recycled Foam Foundation
	FSC certified Wood
Renewable Energy:	6.8 kW PV

Eastern Wall in Gallery

Southern Wall in ADU

LIVING **BUILDING** CHALLENGE & LIVING **COMMUNITY** CHALLENGE

Rooted Investing LLC is choosing to register the Emerson Street House LLC for the International Living Future Institute's (ILFI): Living Building Challenge (LBC) because ILFI uses a systems approach. A flower, with seven Petals.

Energy | Water | Materials

Place | Equity | Health & Happiness | Beauty & Inspiration

These last four Petals are the most important Petals, fully integrating ILFI's mission with building science.

Emerson St House has been recognized in the **Pacific Northwest Passive House 2016 Magazine** for its performance of

Heating energy	6.7 kBtu/ft²/yr
Heating load	3.1 Btu/ft²/hr
Cooling energy	NA
Total source energy	32.5 kBtu/ft²/yr
Air leakage	0.30 ACH_{50}

North East Green Roof

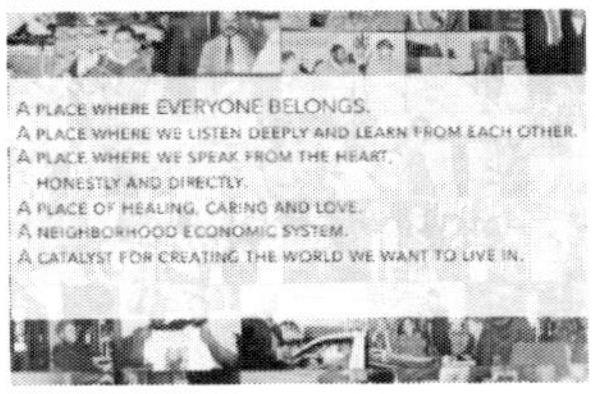

A PLACE WHERE EVERYONE BELONGS.
A PLACE WHERE WE LISTEN DEEPLY AND LEARN FROM EACH OTHER.
A PLACE WHERE WE SPEAK FROM THE HEART, HONESTLY AND DIRECTLY.
A PLACE OF HEALING, CARING AND LOVE.
A NEIGHBORHOOD ECONOMIC SYSTEM.
A CATALYST FOR CREATING THE WORLD WE WANT TO LIVE IN.

THE EMERSON STREET HOUSE IS SACRED SPACE.
HOPE FOR THE FUTURE.

PEACE!

THE EMERSON STREET HOUSE IS FOR SALE

The Emerson Street House is a unique property in the world. Our Volunteer Team considered all aspects of the human existence to create a healthy, happy living environment, incorporating all seven petals of the International Living Future Institute.

Christopher Alexander and Jane Jacobs may not have predicted a pandemic, however, their wisdom in building multi-generational homes that became an integral part of the neighborhood eased the adjustment to remote work and home schooling.

Pandemic lockdowns forced everyone to rethink their living arrangements. Home immediately became Work / Live / Eat / Play / Pray for most families and individuals. As the lockdowns dragged on from weeks to months to years, folks started to evaluate how they wanted to live their lives. The Emerson Street House is laid out perfectly for the post lockdown world.

Jen Sotolongo, BGI Classmate, Blogger and Photographer, produced a Realtor's Tour of the Emerson Street House as it was when I lived there. Since then, the Emerson Street House has had a series of caretakers, each adding their touch.

Soon the Emerson Street House will transition to a family of five, who we hope will live there for a very long time.

THE ACCESSORY DWELLING UNIT (ADU)

Our Team learned quite after the fact that only skinny houses were allowed on the lot at 1006 NE Emerson Street so The Emerson Street House is considered a single-family home with five bedrooms and three baths. But I digress, this is our team's vision of the Emerson Street House.

The ADU was built for me to Age at Home. I have Charcot-Marie-Tooth, a disease that I was born with, inherited from my mother. My feet were increasingly painful and I need surgery to alleviate the pain. Dr. Elliott Michael DPM, Broadway Foot and Ankle, and I were discussing the procedure and the need for six to eight weeks bed rest with my foot elevated.

The ADU Kitchen

The ADU Kitchen was designed, according to Christopher Alexander, as a space that could change over time, accommodating a small family, teenage children, or elders. At the time, I lived alone and would not have any live-in help after my surgery. Neighbors would bring groceries, I could cook, do laundry, etc., by myself.

Out team chose IKEA Business Portland for the kitchen. IKEA seems to have gone downhill since then, perhaps because of the material shortages caused by the pandemic, a real shame since IKEA worked so well at The Emerson Street House.

The interior wall of the ADU is the kitchen. The cost was 20% of the cost of traditional cabinets and provided four times the storage.

First the panorama view of the great room, living room, dining room, kitchen, laundry, office, community meeting room...

Next IKEA drawers and storage...

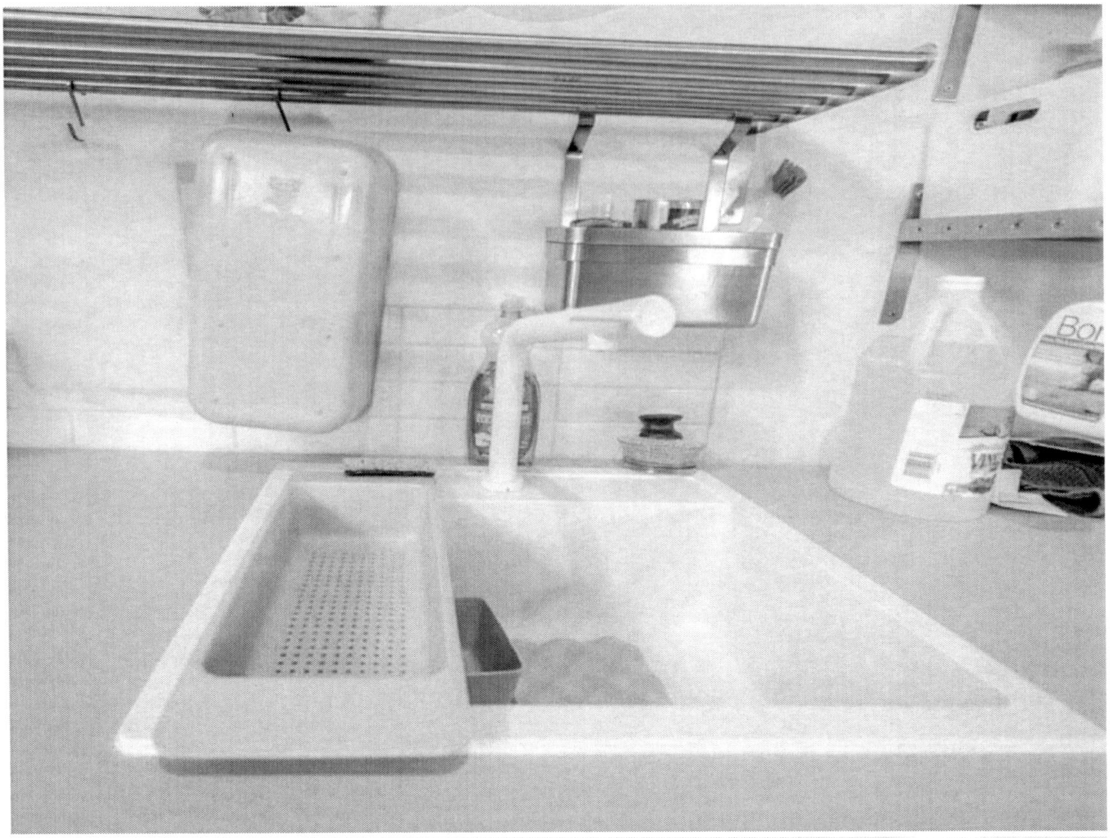

Natural Directions
ORGANIC
Coconut Milk

The ADU Master Bedroom

Next, my bedroom, well hidden behind the privacy wall and next to the bathroom. I share my bedroom with Daphne, my grand dog, and family photos. My neighbor, Joanne Suell Green, gifted me the quilt on my bed, it is 300 years old and quilted by hand. The small quilt over my bed was quilted by Joanne Suell Green (Joanne's Quilts).

The Other ADU Bedroom

Whoops! It's missing. I think we were hiding the junk in there so Jen Sotolongo could get the good happy pictures for the realtor's tour.

The ADU Bathroom

The bathroom next to my bedroom—not handicap accessible, but the best we could do in a small space.

"Love Mother Earth". Mini-mural created by Sharon Koskoff, the Duchess of Deco, for my birthday gift.

Cedar plank floor looks cool, looks can be deceiving.

The ADU Backyard Garden

Backyard garden as seen from the back of the great room. Great in the summer, not so great in the rainy season and the snow.

The ADU Accessible Entrance

The accessible entrance to the ADU, with my signature quote "I'm Done with This Conservation." Sign created by Wynde Dyer, Multi-Media Artist and Master Quilter.

THE MAIN HOUSE

View of the Emerson Street House from the Street

"Everyone Belongs," the motto of the Emerson Street House. Sign created by Wynde Dyer, Tarp Quilt and Eclectic Artist.

"A Book Is A Dream You Can Hold in Your Hand," Neil Gaiman, alongside the Accessible Staircase up to the Main House and ADU Entrances to The Emerson Street House. In Gratitude to Muffie Delgado Connelly for the inspirational quote.

The Main House Entrance

The Main House Entrance is at the top of the accessible staircase and to the right, abutting the ADU window. Wynde Dyer's Tarp Quilts accent the cedar plank exterior.

The front view of the Main House Entrance.

Emerson House Mail Box, complete with live roof garden and solar panels which light the windows, designed and installed by Emily Wobb, Portland Artist.

The Main House Roof Garden

The Main House Roof Garden is up the stairs and to the right. We will fly right up and out the door, leaving the inside until last. These photos were taken just after the City Repair event at the Emerson Street House, while their nest was still partially up.

The Main House Staircase

The Main House Kitchen and Laundry Room

IKEA kitchen and laundry room under the staircase

Moroccan tea service by Ovations Coffee Shop in the Pearl District

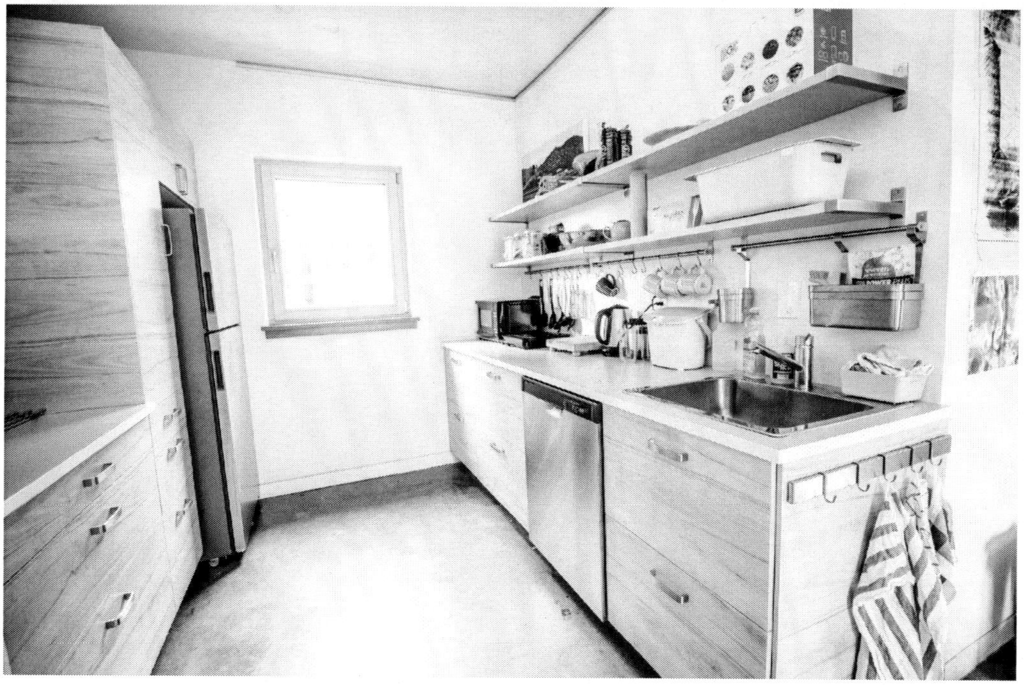

The Main House Great Room

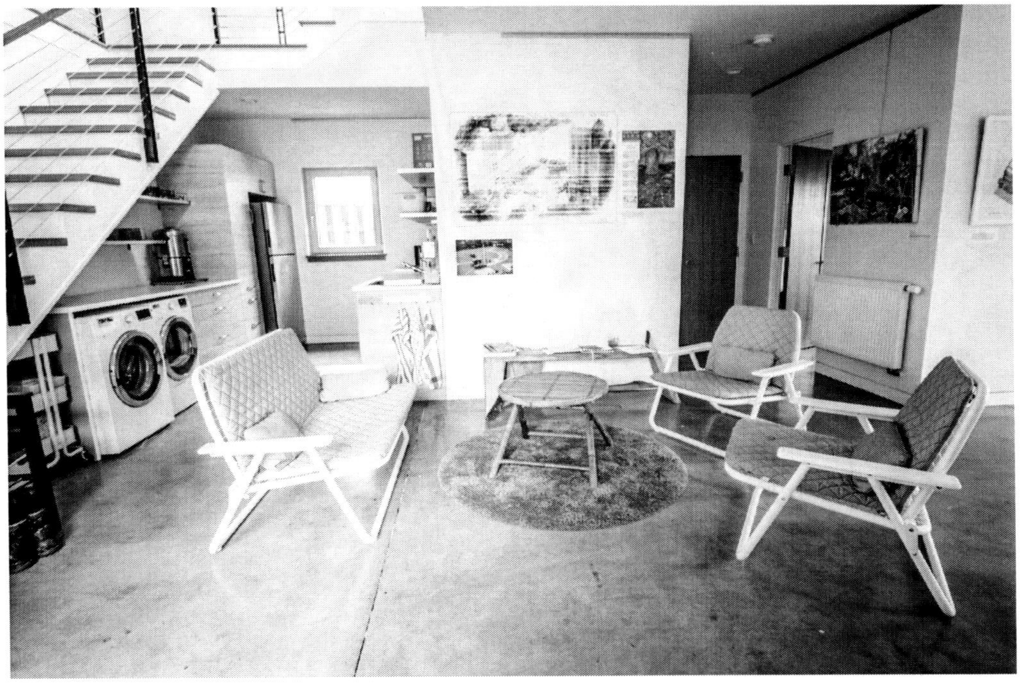

Sitting area for Bonnie Meltzer (very mixed media) Exhibit on Making Electricity

Mommy
Time-out
Daddy
Time-out
I LOVE COLORS!
I'm not a book worm, I'm a book dragon
The Curious Garden
VISTAS of MANY WORLDS
Reading gives us some places to go when we have to stay where we are
I Love My Hair!
An Apple
I Did it!
Did it!
Full of LOVE
Between the pages of a book is a lovely place to be
¿Quién Teme
¡FIESTA!
LAROUSSE
A library is full of new worlds to travel

The Main House Downstairs Bedroom

The Main House Downstairs Bathroom

The Main House Upstairs Apartment

The upstairs apartment includes two bedrooms, a bath, and a private sitting area.

Upstairs sitting area, with a folding out couch for guests.

Upstairs Master Bedroom

RESOURCES

Introduction to Resources

In my other eBooks, I listed articles and other media that informed my work.

Jane Jacob's was so prolific and so profound that I would waste hours documenting what others have so elegantly documented. **The Death and Life of Great American Cities**, written in 1961 is still the bible of urban planning today. The pandemic has created challenges for new theories of urban planning. Jane Jacobs, if she were still among us, would say poppycock - we just adjust. Our new reality – Work / Live / Eat / Pray / Pray. Initially forced into remote work by pandemic lockdown, folks have embraced remote work and no longer want to commute to an office environment, no matter how grand the office.

Christopher Alexander anticipated different uses for towns and buildings during different phases of folks' lifecycle. I tried to follow his lead, but often missed the mark. I moved back to Florida, where I belong and am allowing the Emerson Street House to evolve into the place it was met to be.

Wikipedia

Wikipedia my go-to place for factual information or at least it was until I read this article from Wikipedia co-founder Larry Sanger, Wikipedia Is Badly Biased, (https://larrysanger.org/2020/05/wikipedia-is-badly-biased/).

Now I am really paranoid and may have to adopt Cheryl Strayed's ***Wild***, "Every effort has been made to trace or contact all copyright holders. The publishers will be pleased to make good any omissions or rectify any mistakes brought to their attention at the earliest opportunity." (Source: Reedsyblog, https://blog.reedsy.com/copyright-page)

Jason F. McLennan | Canadian | Born, Sudbury Ontario https://en.wikipedia.org/wiki/Jason_F._McLennan

Bullitt Foundation | Capital Hill, Seattle Washington | Certified as a Living Building by the International Living Future Institute https://en.wikipedia.org/wiki/Bullitt_Center

Christopher Alexander | American/British | Trinity, Cambridge, Harvard, MIT https://en.wikipedia.org/wiki/Christopher_Alexander

Jane Jacobs | American/ Canadian | Journalist, author, urban theorist https://en.wikipedia.org/wiki/Jane_Jacobs

Marisa Zylkowski (Hagney) Sustainability | Architecture | Design https://www.linkedin.com/in/marisazylkowski/

Books

Alexander, Christopher et al (Sara Ishikawa, Murry Silverstein with Max Jacobson, Ingrid Fiksdahl-King, Shlomo Angel). **A Pattern Language: Towns, Buildings, Construction**. Oxford University Press (New York). 1977.

Brookins, Cara. **Rise: How a House Built a Family.** St. Martin's Press (New York). 2017.

Jacobs, Jane. **The Death and Life of Great American Cities**. New York: Random House, 1961.

ACKNOWLEDGEMENTS

In Gratitude

To Nicole Sandoval aka Nikki Brown Clown for her dedication to provide culturally specific books for all children and for promoting home schooling as an important alternative for all children.

To Guillermo Sandoval, Community Banker, for supporting his wife Nikki Brown Clown and the local Community through his work at Tri-County and Umpqua Banks. Special recognition to Guillermo and Nikki for their work with the children and teachers displaced by the Camp Fire in Paradise California

To Kali Amanda Browne for teaching me the art and science of self-publishing books and improving the quality of my writing dramatically.

To Nicholas Papaefthimiou for his support through the years as I learned about the build environment, the culture of northeast Portland and as investment partner in affordable housing.

To Mia Sheperd and Irish Gomm for their spunk and drive and support of the Emerson Street House.

REAL PEOPLE

Professionals who Volunteered their Time and Expertise to Complete the Living Building Challenge / Living Community Challenge

My mind is boggled as I think of all the people who have blessed the Emerson Street House. Some folks prefer to remain anonymous, which I want to respect. If you are not on the list, I have decided that you are among the many folks who like to work quietly in the background.

Felecia Hatcher and Derick Pearson, Black Tech Week, Miami

Kadi McLean, McLean Brand Development (Marketing Maven)

Nicholas Papaefthimiou, AIA, LEED BD+C, Architect and Structural Engineer, MIT, UC Berkeley, Investor and Developer of Affordable Housing, Founder Infill PDX

Cory Huff, The Abundant Artist

Muffie Delgado Connelly, Dancer

Robin Corbo, Muralist

Mark Lakeman, Grassroots Urban Placemaking

Kirk Rhea, City Repair

Mia Sheperd, Cal Poly (Architecture and Environmental Design)

Irish Gomm, Cal Poly (Architecture and Environmental Design)

Ky Burt, Singer/ Songwriter and Music Therapist

Tommy Blockson, Dog Walker Extraordinaire and Emerson Street neighbor

Kevin Beasley, Multimedia Journalist, University of Oregon, Navy Veteran

Zach Putnam, ZPproductions, Filmmaker, Producer, Head Cheerleader

Joanne Suell Green, Emerson Street neighbor and Joanne's Quilts

Vanessa White, Emerson Street neighbor, entrepreneur, and model parent, grandparent, and homeowner.

S. Renee Mitchell, Renaissance Woman and Teacher Extraordinaire

Activists and Visionaries

Christopher Alexander - From his Amazon Author's Page

For nearly 50+ years Christopher Alexander has challenged the architectural establishment, sometimes uncomfortably, to pay more attention to the human beings at the center of design. To do so he has combined top-flight scientific training, award-winning architectural research, patient observation and testing throughout his building projects, and a radical but profoundly influential set of ideas that have extended far beyond the realm of architecture.

In the process Alexander has authored a series of groundbreaking works, including **A Pattern Language: Towns, Buildings, Construction and The Timeless Way of Building**. His most recent publication continues that ground-breaking work, the four-volume book set, **The Nature of Order: An Essay on the Art of Building and the Nature of the Universe**, incorporates more than 30 years of research, study, teaching and building. It was described by Laura Miller of the New York Times" the kind of book every serious reader should wrestle with once in a while: [a] fat, challenging, grandiose tract that encourages you to take apart the way you think and put it back together again."

Alexander was born in Vienna, Austria and raised in Oxford and Chichester, England. He was awarded the top open scholarship to Trinity College, Cambridge in 1954, in chemistry and physics, and went on to read mathematics at Cambridge. He took his doctorate in architecture at Harvard (the first Ph.D. in architecture ever awarded at Harvard), and was elected to the society of Fellows at Harvard University in 1961. During the same period, he worked at MIT in transportation theory and in computer science, and at Harvard in cognitive science. His pioneering ideas from that time were known to be highly influential in those fields.

Alexander became Professor of Architecture at the University of California, Berkeley in 1963, and taught there continuously for 38 years, becoming Professor Emeritus in 2001. He founded the Center for Environmental Structure in 1967, published hundreds of papers and several dozen books, and built more than 200 buildings around the world.

Alexander is widely recognized as the father of the pattern language movement in computer science, which has led to important innovations such as Wiki, and new kinds of Object-Oriented Programming. He is the recipient of the first medal for research ever given by the American Institute of Architects, and he has been honored repeatedly for his buildings in many parts of the world. He was elected Fellow of the American Academy of Arts and Sciences in 1996 for his contributions to architecture, including his groundbreaking work on how the built environment affects the lives of people.

Jane Jacobs - From her Amazon Author's Page

Thirty years after its publication, **The Death and Life of Great American Cities** was described by the New York Times as "perhaps the most influential single work in the history of town planning.... [It] can also be seen in a much larger context. It is, first, a work of literature; the descriptions of street life as a kind of ballet and the bitingly satiric account of traditional planning theory can still be read for pleasure even by those who long ago absorbed and appropriated the book's arguments." Jane Jacobs, an editor and writer on architecture in New York City in the early sixties, argued that urban diversity and vitality were being destroyed by powerful architects and city planners. Rigorous, sane, and delightfully epigrammatic, Jacobs's small masterpiece is a blueprint for the humanistic management of cities. It is sensible, knowledgeable, readable, indispensable.

From one regret is that Jane Jacobs and I did not meet in person. I lived in New York City around the time Jane Jacobs was living in Greenwich Village and battling Robert Moses. I was busy being good little girl accountant and did not understand the gravity of her work at the time.

Cara Brookins - From her Amazon Author's Page

"Cara Brookins is professional speaker based in Little Rock and is best known for being the mom who built her own house using YouTube tutorials. She has been entertaining, educating, and inspiring audiences with her keynotes and presentations since 2004. She is the author of eight books, including **Rise, how a House Built a Family**, which tells the story of building her 3500 square foot house with the help of her four children by watching YouTube tutorials and googling things like foundation work, plumbing, and gas lines. News of Cara's family story went viral in more than 65 countries and was viewed a billion times. **Rise**, has now been optioned to become a major motion picture. Inspiring audiences to build bigger lives remains her greatest passion."

My one regret is that Cara Brookins 'book was published after The Emerson Street House was completed.

Lina Minard - From Whitman College | Whitman Magazine February 2016

"When you see her in her own house, The Lucky Penny, you're witnessing a form of connection between a maker and an object that's rare in this era. In this way, the homes that Menard facilitates are not possessions, but are possessed with the personalities and utterly unique living tendencies of their owners."

BGIers (Faculty and Students, Bainbridge Graduate Institute)

John Gardner

John taught the **Food and Agriculture Certificate** program the second year of my BGI MBA Program. John was incredibly generous with his time. John was also BGI Dean and battling a rare form of cancer which ultimately resulted in his passing the year after we graduated.

Jimmy Jia

Jimmy Jia taught the **Green Energy Certificate** program the second year of my BGI MBA This is Jimmy's bio from The Jia Group website:

"Jimmy Jia, Managing Partner, grew up within walking distance to the ocean and forests of Central California, where he learned the value of environmental stewardship early on. As an entrepreneur, author, and strategist, he uses energy as an indicator of corporate governance and strategy responsibly manage consumption of natural resources.

Currently, he is a Venture Partner Advisor at PiLabs, sits on the board for the Center for Sustainable Energy and is a Visiting Scholar at George Washington University. It was in his latest book, the **Corporate Energy Strategist's Handbook**, that he proposed the Energy Statements as a metrics framework for improving management of energy resources for better climate outcomes.

He received his BS and MS from the Massachusetts Institute of Technology, and an MBA from the University of Oxford. Read his personal reflection on his energy path: **20 Years Later**."

Jason F. McLennan

Jason taught the **Green Build Certificate** program the second year of my BGI MBA in Sustainable System. Read Jason's bio from the International Living Future Institute, Immediate Past Chair at https://living-future.org/people/jason-f-mclennan/.

"Jason is one of the world's most influential individuals in the field of architecture and the green building movement. He is the winner of the Buckminster Fuller Prize, the National Award of Excellence

Winner from Engineering News Record, a senior fellow of the Design Futures Council and the Ashoka Foundation. He is the creator of the **Living Building Challenge**, **Living Community Challenge**, Living Product Challenge, JUST Social Justice Label, Declare and the Living Future Institute, and is the author of six books on sustainability and green building. He is an architect and planner at **McLennan Design** (his own firm) and currently designing some of the most leading-edge green building projects anywhere."

Stuart Cowan

Stuart Cowan taught the **Local Living Economies** program the second year of my BGI MBA in Sustainable Systems. Stuart is currently EVP and Chief Scientist at Santa Fe Farms.

From Stuart Cowan's LinkedIn page:

"Santa Fe Farms has positioned itself to become a preeminent leader in Industrial Hemp and important hemp products such as paper and pulp, animal and human proteins, and bioplastics."

THE ADU AT THE EMERSON STREET HOUSE

What Is an Accessory Dwelling Unit (ADU)?

Investopedia defines ADU as:

"An accessory dwelling unit (ADU) is a legal and regulatory term for a secondary house or apartment that shares the building lot of a larger, primary home. The unit cannot be bought or sold separately, but they are often used to provide additional income through rent or to house a family member. For example, an elderly parent could live in a small unit and avoid having to move to an assisted living facility."

ADU Study by the Oregon Department of Environmental Studies

Lina Minard, Niche Consulting founder/owner/operator, Whitman College, Class of 2005, was evidently hired by the Oregon Department of Environmental to conduct a study of ADU in Portland Oregon. This is ADU Case Study that I submitted to Lina

The ADU at the Emerson Street House

Quick Facts

Setting: Urban – Northeast Portland

Neighborhood: King Neighborhood, Northeast Portland, OR

Type: New Construction – Main House and ADU

ADU Use: Diane Freaney's Live/Work/Studio Space

Square Footage: 798 SF

Year Built: Certificate of Occupancy Issued May 2, 2016

Owner: Emerson Street House LLC, an Oregon Benefits Company, single-member Diane Freaney

Designer: Jeff Stern, In Situ Architecture, Certified Passive House Consultant

Original Builder: Original Design Build Firm has resigned from the project

Original Builder Cost: $376,325.70 ($471.59 per SF)

Replicable Cost: $160,000 ($200.00 per SF)

In June 2013, Diane graduated from Bainbridge Graduate Institute (BGI) (now merged with Presidio) with an MBA in Sustainable

Systems. The second-year curriculum changed the focus of Diane's work from Wall Street investing to rooted investing – Local Living Economies (Stuart Cowan), Green Build (Jason McLennan), Energy (Jimmy Jia) and Food and Agriculture (John Gardner).

After graduation, Diane connected with Lise and Steve Monohan, goat farmers from Gales Creek, Oregon. Lise wrote to BGI asking for help in securing financing for a new dairy barn. Lise and Steve purchased Fraga Farms, a well-respected local goat cheese maker. The Fraga goats had to be moved from Sweet Home, Oregon to Gales Creek. The local bank turned Lise and Steve down for a $100,000 loan. Their farm appraised at $500,000, with a $90,000 mortgage, a 15-year mortgage AND they had never missed a payment. Lise had a full-time job as a public health nurse. AND Lise and Steve owned 3 investment properties, single-family homes in Portland, all rented at below market rates, which more than covered the mortgage payment, including real estate taxes and insurance.

Lise and Steve decide to sell their property in the Alberta Arts district. They purchased 1006 NE Emerson Street on May 2, 2005, with a 15-year mortgage. The tenant had already given notice that she was moving out at the end of the lease.

Diane just sold all her Wall Street investments and had cash to make local investments. Diane and Lise agreed on a price and closed in August. Lise taught Diane about tiny houses, Accessory Dwelling Units (ADUs), Portland building codes, the history of North and Northeast Portland and the King neighborhood.

Diane's goal was to build at least 2 living units on the property. Diane had a lot to learn and many false starts. She had plans drawn up to renovate the existing house and put a tiny house on the property. Then a renovation and a free standing ADU. Finally, Diane learned there was no other option except to deconstruct the existing structure and start from scratch – the original foundation was built without rebar and the house was riddled with black mold.

Jeff Stern, It Situ Architecture, gave Diane a tour of Skidmore Passivhaus, his family's home, studio, and office in the Cully neighborhood. Jeff built Skidmore Passivhaus using Passive house standards. The building is placed on the property to take maximum advantage of the sun to provide heat in cold months, electric shades to keep the sun out during hot months, thick heavily insulated walls, tight envelope, cement floors, special doors and windows.

Diane decided to build a Passive House, Net Zero house with an attached ADU after her tour of Skidmore Passivhaus. The studio and office wing has a bathroom that Diane replicated in the Emerson Street House. There is currently no kitchen in the studio and office wing so Skidmore Passivhaus is not classified as an ADU. A kitchen could be added if living needs changed.

Smaller spaces, less stuff, shared spaces, and spaces that serve multiple purposes create sustainable, resilient communities. The Emerson Street House was designed to serve many purposes, for now and over time.

The ADU layout is simple – approximately 36' x 25' exterior walls, 798 SF, with 2 bedrooms, 1 bath and a "great room" that includes a kitchen, laundry, living space, studio, and office.

Inspirations for the project were Jane Jacobs, ***The Death and Life of Great American Cities;*** Annie Leonard, ***The Story of Stuff;*** and Theaster Gates, Artist, based on the south side of Chicago. Diane – "My goal was to create community, not just build a building."

To finance the project, Diane reinvested funds from the sale of her condo and used personal funds formerly invested in Wall Street to pay for the balance. Diane's philosophy, ***owning your own home, free of any debt, is the best investment anyone can***

make. Learn how to maintain your home and your home will maintain its value. When your mortgage is paid off, consider adding an ADU and renting it out either on a nightly/weekly basis or affordably to local resident(s) (30% of cash net income for rent and utilities).

Jeff Stern performed the Passive House calculations using the Passive House Planning Package (PHPP), a giant Excel spreadsheet developed by the *Passivhaus Institut* in Germany. The PHPP allows energy modeling and optimization in design. Jeff Stern skill in PHPP modeling gave the Emerson Street House the SIMPLE and structurally efficient design in both the ADU and the MAIN house.

Diane recommends that you hire an independent Architect, even if you will be doing the work yourself. The University of Oregon (UofO) and Portland State University (PSU) both have Architecture programs and may be able to connect you with an Architecture student, if you are concerned about cost.

Nicholas Papaefthimiou, https://www.pdx.edu/architecture/profile/nicholas-papaefthimiou, Adjunct Faculty, PSU and UofO, also builds ADUs which he rents affordably through his company Infill PDX, http://infillpdx.com/who.html.

Diane recommends that you be your own Project Manager for your ADU. The Google definition – "As the project manager, your job is to plan, budget, oversee and document all aspects of the specific project you are working on." The project manager assigned by the builder did not understand his job and the project suffered.

Don't waste time or money on Certifications. Certification is the attempt to verify that a project meets a standard. Earth Advantage issued a Net Zero Certificate dated May 2016, based on a blower test performed in March 2016. The cost of the Certification was $2,700, paid for by "Contractor's Incentive." Earth Advantage only deals with builders AND has refused to meet with Diane.

The best way to record energy data for energy usage for your ADU every month, pay attention to the usage. [Energy Usage Table]. The Emerson Street House ADU is "Net Zero", while the MAIN house is not. Diane, A&R Solar, and a new electrician are diagnosing the situation, with a goal of reaching Net Zero for both the MAIN House and the ADU to meet "Net Zero" standards for the Living Building Challenge of the International Living Future Institute.

The Passive House Institute US (PHIUS) issued a Certificate, dated August 1, 2016, which indicates to Diane that Jeff Stern completed the Certification at the Emerson Street House on August 1, 2016. The Emerson Street House did not meet *Passivhaus Institut* standards that August 1, 2016. The inside temperature was 80 degrees, with still air, no ventilation.

Major design considerations. Diane is 73 years old with Charcot-Marie-Tooth, a neurological disease that affect Diane's strength, balance, and mobility. The ADU is Diane's live/work space, where Diane plans to live and work for the rest of her life.

1. Diane's requirement for no stairs to access the ADU and no stairs inside.

2. Diane wants the ADU to be a public space, where neighbors felt comfortable stopping by and a private space when Diane needs "alone time." The Great Room is visible from the ADU front door. Diane's bedroom, which has a door, is behind the kitchen wall for privacy.

3. Diane is prone to seasonal depression during the dark days of winter. High ceiling and windows without window covering allow maximum light.

4. Diane loves Jane Jacobs concept of "eyes on the street." Place a window facing the street where the resident will stand

frequently, for example the kitchen. The resident will watch the coming and going of folks, including children, and become an unofficial "safe streets program". Diane wanted the ADU front window to allow Diane to see the street. The window is set too high so Diane has to stand outside the front door to see the street. This is high on Diane's list to correct.

The Emerson Street House, both MAIN house and ADU, was designed for multi-generational living and Aging at Home. Diane's inspiration came from her parent's end of life residency in Assisted Living. The primary caregivers - Certified Nursing Assistants (CNAs) were primarily young mothers. Every morning the CNAs left their children with neighbors, family or friends and drove to the Assisted Living facility, carpooling with neighbors if possible. The CNAs spent the day with cranky, bored old people, with little to look forward to, all the while worrying about their own children.

Diane's parents hated Assisted Living and only wanted to be in their own home. Diane thought – what if houses were designed to allow caregivers and their families to live in a residence with the folks they took care of. The Main house was designed with a master bedroom on the first floor, with an accessible bathroom right outside the bedroom door. Upstairs there are two bedrooms, one bath, a sitting area and access to the roof patio and the eco-roof.

Diane reasons that a senior who wants to stay in their home could trade room and board with a young family. The partners could arrange for one partner to be at home as needed by the senior. The partners would cook, clean, and do laundry for the senior as part of their daily routine of caring for their own family. One partner (or both if they had different schedules) could work outside the home, keeping all earnings to provide for their own families, perhaps saving to purchase their own home in the future.

Diane plans to live in the ADU until she passes. The second

bedroom would be available for a caregiver to live-in if Diane needs help. Caregivers could work together to give each more freedom to spent time with their families.

The quality of life for the seniors improves when they stay in their homes with the things they love and their memories AND they have the social life and connection they need because they are part of a young family's life. The reality is that this type of arrangement happens all the time in low-income families because low-income families can't afford Assisted Living.

If Diane had it to do over again, there are seven things Diane would do differently.

1. Diane would hire an independent Architect. Diane would meet with the Architect weekly, either in person or on Skype or cell, during the planning, permitting, and building stage. Then quarterly for at least two years after the Certificate of Occupancy is issued to diagnose and correct construction defects, if any.

2. Diane would visit the Bureau of Development Services with the Architect so she understood the permitting process, code issues and how to advocate for her own ideas.

3. Diane would insist on Hammer & Hand's project model of Three Advocates https://hammerandhand.com/about/designer-builder-client/a collaborative process between Architect, Builder and Client to design and construct the best response to the project's program.

4. Diane would follow her rooted investing philosophy – DO IT YOURSELF (DIY) - and act as Project Manager.

5. Diane would insist on copies of all documentation on the project, including all materials used, original bids from each sub-contractor, all change orders, copies of all bills, and verification of payments, before paying each progress billing.

6. Diane would assemble her own Home Manual, containing all Maintenance Manuals, documentation of materials used, all accounting documentation from every subcontractor and anything else pertinent to the ADU.

7. Finally, in any building project there can and will be mistakes. The mark of true professionals is how they craft a solution. Diane would make sure she asked about failures and how the professional handled the failure. Diane would NOT sign a contract with a builder or architect that said they never had a failure or blamed someone else for their failure.

So, what advice does Diane have for homeowners considering creating an ADU on their own property?

Take a DIY approach, even if you will not be doing the building yourself.

Read ***Rise: How A House Built a Family*** by Cara Brookins. Cara and her four children built a five-bedroom house, using YouTube instructional videos and occasional additional help that seemed to show up at critical times. The one "professional" Cara hired – a licensed and bonded electrician – created more problems that they (both men) solved.

Talk to friends, colleagues and acquaintance who have built and ask about their experience.

Go on ADU tours and just walk around your neighborhood, looking to see if you can spot already existing ADUs. Talk to your neighbors. Ask them how they like ADUs in their neighborhood – or do they even notice.

Be clear about your values and your reasons for building an ADU. For example, Airbnb might seem like a cash cow, until you understand that you are a host, which takes time, and your UNIT may be empty in winter months. Perhaps renting a family at 30% of their income for rent and utilities, will be a better option, if the family will provide maintenance for the ADU and the garden.

E-mail thecatlady@dianefreaney.com to schedule a tour of the ADU at the Emerson Street House. Diane made many mistakes AND she is happy to share her mistakes and her solutions to correct the construction defects.

Other possible things to include:

How do the residents of the ADU and main house interact?

Right now, the MAIN house operates as a community space with an Artist-In-Residency program, the Nikki Brown Clown Free Library, House Concerts, an Art Gallery, and community meetings and events. Donovan Smith, DIY Artist-In-Residency Program Director lives in one of the 3 rooms, with the other two rooms available for Artists.

Diane lives in the ADU with Daphne, her grand dog, a 13-year-old Wheaten Terrier. Diane and Donovan usually meet daily to catch up and perhaps share a meal. Both live and work in the same space so there are business and personal reasons to interact.

Do you feel you have adequate storage in your ADU?

Kitchen – The builder installed kitchen was so poorly designed, Diane was forced to think about kitchens differently. Diane realized that she was only using the oven as a toaster, which heated up the already overheated ADU. And if the oven went away, there was no need for a Hood, which took up precious wall space needed for shelves. The Induction Cooktops never worked and there was no need for a Garbage Disposal because Diane composts.

Diane made an appointment with the kitchen planning department at IKEA, which Diane discovered is THE go-to place for kitchens today. Diane uninstalled both the ADU and the MAIN builder installed kitchens, ordered, and installed IKEA kitchens that cost 10% of the cost of builder installed kitchens, tripled the storage space, and left room to include the washer/dryer and a recycling center in the kitchen footprint.

Closets - The only purpose for closets with doors is to hide the mess. In an ADU, which has a smaller footprint, closet doors also get in the way and make the space seem even smaller. A sustainable solution is to have everything neatly stored in plain sight on shelves and/or hanging on racks. Everything that doesn't fit goes in the free box on the sidewalk. Both IKEA and Storables have inexpensive closet systems that work well.

Diane's only regret is that the builder did not listen when Diane told them that she did NOT want closets at all. "Closets in bedroom are code," said the builder. Diane's response - "The code is outdated. How do we change the code?"

The electrical and the plumbing subcontractors seemed to be confused by the closets also because we found electric wires and plumbing pipes in the strangest places.

What sustainability features were included?

Solar panels on the roof, permeable cement on the driveway, an eco-roof on the MAIN house, and many more. Diane is still working to get complete documentation on materials used from the original Design Build firm and will share complete information as soon as it is available.

Diane is drawn to the philosophy of the International Living Future Institute...

What if every single act of design and construction made the world a better place?

The Living Building Challenge is the world's most

rigorous proven performance standard for buildings. People from around the world use our regenerative design framework to create spaces that, like a flower, give more than they take.

ILFI's Seven Petals are PLACE, EQUITY, HEALTH & HAPPINESS, BEAUTY & INSPIRATION and materials, energy, and water. The Emerson Street Team has focused on the Petals all in Caps, the People-Oriented Petals. People, not buildings, create sustainability through creativity, curiosity, and behavior.

There is no one right answer for using materials, energy, and water sustainably. The best sustainability solution right now is a stepping stone to a better solution in the future. Our world is a system and constantly changing as systems do. The only truly detrimental action to creating a sustainable project is "status quo."

The Emerson Street House is registered for the Living Building Challenge and the Emerson Street Community, a neighborhood collective, is registered for the Living Community Challenge, two programs of the International Living Future Institute.

How well is the ADU serving your needs?

Diane loves living in the ADU. She unlocks the door in the morning and has a stream of neighbors and business appointments in and out all day long. The ADU is the perfect space to support her work with rooted investing, connecting local organizations and Oregonians with local investing opportunities. The best way to serve the local community is to become part of the community. Too often we look to outside experts for guidance, when the answers are within ourselves and our communities.

What has surprised you about having an ADU on your property?

The most common question about the Emerson Street House –

What is this place?

What do you like best about having an ADU on your property?

All aspects of my life are integrated. I am rooted in my neighborhood for the first time in my life.

What's your favorite feature of your ADU? What are you most proud of?

Great windows and doors that provide good light even in the darkest days of winter. The ADU provides enough privacy by the way it sits on the property so that shades and drapes in the winter are not necessary.

Do you have a website detailing your experience?

Check out the What Is This Place? book series on Diane's Amazon Author's Page www.amazon.com/author/dianefreaney

My web site is www.dianefreaney.com

Anything else you'd like to share?

Portland has many creative, inspiring folks and organizations working to build sustainable, resilient communities. The Emerson Street House is honored to be participating in that process.

2018 UNCONFERENCE IN PORTLAND, OREGON

My letter to Jason McLennan, Board Chair, International Living Future Institute, says it all. Jason McLennan never ever acknowledged that he received my letter and certainly did not share it with his Board as I asked him to do.

Julie Tonroy is still the Director - Events for ILFI. Why not? She gets paid by the number of warm bodies she brings in the door. But times they are changing. Events are online, not in person. Some of the best online events are FREE.

EMERSON ST. HOUSE

Emerson Street House LLC, an Oregon Benefits Company

1006 NE Emerson Street UNIT B, Portland, OR 97211323-632-6638

diane@emersonstreethouse.com

January 27, 2018

Jason McClellan Board Chair

International Living Future Institute

1501 E Madison Street, Suite 150, Seattle WA 98122

RE: The Emerson Street Community, a registered project of the Living Community Challenge

Dear Jason,

I was an MBA student at during 2012-2013, the year you taught Green Building at Bainbridge Graduate Institute. I was inspired by your vision, attended ILFI's 2014 unConference in Portland, Oregon, met some folks who said they could build a Passive, Net Zero house and built the Emerson Street House.

Murthys Srinivas, fellow BGI Alum, an ILFI/Social Venture Partner volunteer, introduced me to Marisa Hagney and convinced me to register for the Living Community Challenge, and the Living Building Challenge.

I am flabbergasted that Julie Tonroy never contacted us for our input and to ask us what we wanted to present for the 2018 unConference May 1-4, 2018. The Emerson Street Community is the:

- Only project registered for the Living Community Challenge in Portland, Oregon
- Only project (out of 14 in the world) with people on its landing page, NXNE: The Skanner Photography of Julie Keefe, 1991-2008
- Only project in an historically Black/Indian (or Native American) neighborhood that was hijacked and decimated by the Oregon white population
- Only grassroots funded project, all expenses paid from my retirement income
- Only project staffed by all volunteers
- Only project focused on community as people, not buildings - Jane Jacobs, The Death and Life of Great American Cities

Nicholas Papaefthimiou contacted Alicia Uhlig and Marisa Hagney, who passed our information on to Julie Tonroy. Julie gave this response, paraphrased by Nicholas –

The presentation slots are filled, as are all the tours. I suggested we could host one of the after parties or something at the Emerson house but she thinks they need to cancel some of their evening socials as it is... too many venues, and frankly, not enough interest.

I drove by the South Waterfront the other day and I thought –

Robert Moses has won. There are so many brand-new badly built buildings in Portland today, so many vacancies, so many houseless children and families, so many stressed our renters and owners that need housing which really is affordable. There are so many pressing issues which the unConference could have addressed. Julie is focused on how much money she can extract and who our team can introduce her to.

I am pretty disgusted right now. JasonMclennan.com: "We can design Living Buildings instead of buildings that degrade our communities." Do you actually believe this or is this greenwashing?

Please have my letter read into the minutes at a full ILFI Board. I would also appreciate a written response that I can share with our team.

In my opinion, ILFI needs a new business model in order to fulfill its mission - OUR IMPACT –

SOCIALLY JUST, CULTURALLY RICH,
ECOLOGICALLY RESTORATIVE

We are premised on the belief that providing a compelling vision for the future is a fundamental requirement for reconciling humanity's relationship with the natural world.

Peace & Love,

DF

Cc: Nicholas Papaefthimiou, Project Manager, LBC/LCC

Mia Sheperd, Project Manager, LBC/LCC

Murthy Srinivas, Wise Adviser

Jimmy Jia, Energy Mentor

EPILOGUE

I have moved back to Florida where I belong. The Emerson Street House will transition soon to a new family.

Chronologically this seems like the perfect place for an epilogue but I have no idea what to say. The books about the Construction Process are still in process and the evolution of the art and cultural dynamics continue to happen.

Thank you for your readership. I hope you have enjoyed the journey.

Author's Bio

Diane Freaney, image from Message to a President by Julie Keefe

I have been seated at the table – rather, more accurately, been seated behind the white men seated at the table and told to hold my tongue – at the launch of some of the most radical new business models of the last century.

I have had a front row seat for every new finance and/or economic theory that came down the pike.

This is a dubious honor. I have watched these same new business models crash and burn, take jobs, destroy families, make ghost towns of cities, compromise our health and well-being, and rob us of our happiness. With the economic meltdown of 2008, I watched as my retirement fund plummeted 42% percent from the top of the market in 2007 to the bottom in 2009.

My life has been magical. I have over 70 years life/work experience and an excellent educational background.

Syracuse University (1965) – In my Accounting courses, I learned to fill in forms and play games with numbers. In Anthropology and Public Speaking, I learned storytelling and gained an appreciation of other cultures.

Harvard Business School – Corporate Finance Executive Education (1982) – I learned about OPM (Other People's Money), the strategy that brought the Global Financial Markets to their knees in 2008.

University of Pennsylvania – Organizational Dynamics (1999) – I learned that student's work is only valued when it follows a structured academic path. My Master's thesis – **A New Model for the Creative Use of College Endowments to Reduce College Tuition** would have prevented today's student loan crisis. Penn had no mechanism for "the administrators" to listen to students.

Bainbridge Graduate Institute (BGI) (2013) – I learned the importance of social media to listening deeply and delivering my message.

At an early age, I learned to communicate by listening. At my current age, I feel driven to share the knowledge and understanding amassed during my lifetime. Now I am speaking out.

—Diane Freaney, The Cat Lady

Coming Soon!
Four Book Series!

What is This Place?

The **What is This Place?** book series includes the final documentation of the Living Building Challenge and the Living Community Challenge of the International Living Future Institute.

This series will include multimedia presentations of events in the Emerson Street Community, including videos and podcasts from The Snarky Express YouTube Channel.

Higher Education

The **Higher Education** book series features the final projects for my graduate degree programs. I have been studying the business of higher education for over sixty years, since I was a teenager researching colleges and universities to decide where I wanted to attend. As you may be able to guess, I have strong opinions on how to bring higher education into this century.

Sally Sleuth will join the team to ferret out political lies and corruption in the higher education systems, focusing on USC, the Ivy League Colleges and Universities, and the State of Florida College and University system. Stay tuned as we dig deep on one of the biggest scandals of our time.

Complexity = Corruption

The **Complexity = Corruption** series was inspired by a Time Magazine article (Complexity Equals Corruption, Fareed Zakaria, Time Magazine, Oct. 31, 2011). The article is about the Complexity of the US Tax Code, of which Zakaria says, "The U.S. tax system is not simply corrupt; it is corrupt in a deceptive manner that has degraded the entire system of American government."

In this series we will explore corruption in Big Tech, Big Pharma, Big everything and anything. The solution is always SIMPLE. I promise a wild ride.

Politics of Place

The **Politics of Place** series started with places I have lived since I was a baby. I have delved into old family photos, photos on the Internet, and stories in my head to fill in the blanks.

Sally Sleuth will be an active partner in this series, since it is peppered with political lies and vested interests. I will leave it to Sally to work on these issues.

I will start with the Surfside Condo Tragedy in Miami-Dade since that has raised the consciousness of all Floridians and change has already started to happen. Condo living is bread and butter for everyone from low income to the wealthiest wealthy.

We Want to Hear from You

Let us know your thoughts.

Email: thecatlady@dianefreaney.com

Or Snail Mail:

Diane Freaney

Emerson House Press

2336 SE Ocean Blvd #230

Stuart, FL 34996-3310

Made in United States
North Haven, CT
06 November 2026

21793613R00048